Love Those Animals

And Be True to Yourself

By Rose Klopf Tithof

Illustrated by Carilyn Teichman

I0173421

Copyright 2021 by Rose Klopf Tithof
All rights reserved.
ISBN# 978-0-9891006-5-6
Published by Reading with Rose

This book is dedicated to the main character, Berlin Rose Tithof Hill. Her love of animals, reading, and family is truly depicted in this story. She is my only granddaughter and is loved dearly.

Berlin Rose was destined to be unique. She lived near Los Angeles with her parents, Alle and Matt. Berlin was the happiest when her mom would push her around the L.A. Zoo in her stroller.

As a toddler, Berlin loved watching the small, playful Emperor Tamarin monkeys with their long white whiskers. Her mom told her these monkeys are found in Brazil, Peru, and Bolivia.

Berlin clearly loved animals, and they loved her. The family dogs, Woody and Fletcher, often sniffed around B's bouncy chair, waiting for Berlin's gentle pats.

Other dog friends of Berlin included Lucy, a rescue schnauzer/lab and Norman, a Shih Tzu. She stopped to pet and talk to family and friends' dogs whenever she saw them.

Berlin often lined up the stuffed animals in her room, as if they were in her own little zoo. She talked to the animals and could be heard purring, barking or growling.

Berlin also loved going to The Living Desert Zoo and Gardens with her grandmother, MorMor. They were allowed to feed the giraffes some of their favorite food—leaves of trees and bushes. MorMor explained those lovely spotted creatures only live in Africa… and zoos.

READ

BOYS
Best
Friend

Kids
can
Cook!

FunFish

The Playhouse

FUNNY
JOKES

Cinderella

Z
is for zebra

Spooky
Stories

The
Snowman
Smile

ABC

Animals
A-Z

CAFE

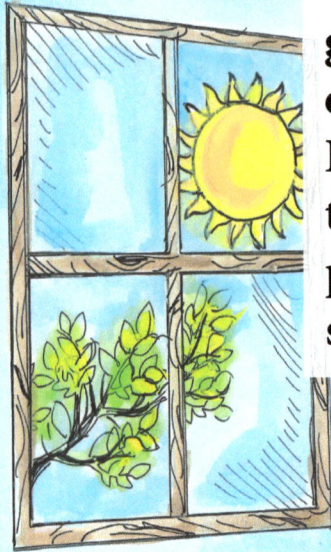

At preschool, while other girls pretended to be princesses or played in the mock kitchen, Berlin could be found pretending to be an animal. She often purred and meowed, with a satisfied cat-grin on her face.

When the preschool teacher noticed that Berlin was not joining in with the other girls, she met with Alle and Matt to express concern. Knowing their daughter's love for animals, they explained, "Berlin often pretends to be an animal at home. Please let her continue with her playacting because that is a big part of who she is."

MiMi visited Berlin's school for Grandparents' Day. On the playground, Mimi saw Berlin hanging upside down on a monkey bar. MiMi asked, "What animal are you today?" Berlin answered very slowly, " a ssssslllllloooooottttthhhh."

While upside down, Berlin said, "Did you know that sloths sleep about 15 hours a day and spend most of their lives upside down?" MiMi smiled as she noticed some of the other students also pretending to be animals.

Berlin's love of animals continued, and she expressed her desire to help them. When her mom told her she could adopt an orphaned elephant through a wildlife trust, Berlin organized a lemonade stand with her brother, Lair, and earned enough money to help a baby elephant for one year.

Receiving emails about her elephant from the Sheldrick Wildlife Trust pleased Berlin. This trust is the world's largest and most successful elephant rescue and rehabilitation program. Berlin loved sharing facts with her brother, "Lair, did you know that elephants are the only animal that can die because of heartbreak?"

THE DAVID SHELDRICK

WILDLIFE TRUST

VISITING STRICTLY

BETWEEN 11-12 NOON

On the day of Berlin's seventh birthday, she rejected the idea of wearing a ruffled dress. "I love shorts and t-shirts," she insisted. And of course, when it was her turn for face-painting, she asked for a cat face.

Berlin's family only had one cat because of her brother's allergies. Their Cornish Rex cat, Winston, had wavy hair and didn't shed much. Because he had such a thin coat, Winnie liked to snuggle. Berlin loved going to friends' houses to play with their cats too.

Berlin and her brother often enjoyed brushing the coats of the Nigerian Dwarf goats in the Petting Kraal at The Living Desert Zoo and Gardens. "Lair, the host told me his name is Patches." Berlin learned the names for all of the goats.

Nigerian Dwarf goats, a rare breed from West Africa, usually weigh 75 pounds and are at most 24 inches tall. Berlin called to Lair, "Do you see how blue his eyes are? They are almost the same color as mine. That is so cool!"

In school, Berlin chose projects about animals whenever she could. For Famous Person Day, Berlin portrayed Jane Goodall, an expert on wild chimpanzees. Berlin told her family, "Today was one of my favorite days at school; I almost felt like I was Dr. Goodall."

Berlin told the other students about Jane Goodall's many discoveries: chimpanzees made tools, hunted for meat, and exhibited some of the same social behaviors as humans. Jane Goodall's favorite was David Greybeard, the chimp who first trusted her and allowed her to come close.

Berlin's family continued to support her love of animals and allowed her to take horseback riding lessons. When Berlin wasn't doing something with animals, she could be found curled up with a good book, as her second love is reading.

By the time Berlin ended first grade, she had read the entire collection of Harry Potter books MiMi had purchased for her. The family would often find B reading one of her favorites, "The Sorcerer's Stone," the first of J.K. Rowling's popular children's novels.

Alle liked to tell Berlin about her basketball days in high school, where she still held a record. Berlin tried to learn some of the skills her mother so badly wanted to teach her. "B, just use your body to box me out…"

Berlin finally told her mom, "Mom, I love how you like basketball so much, but it is just not something I like to do. I have tried. You know what my dream would be? I'd love to write books as well as J.K. Rowling and to live on a farm. Wouldn't that be just the best life?"

Will Berlin achieve her dream? What do you think?

RED
Salutations

BY: AL GLANN

A Lone Horse

I, a lone horse standing in a field,
Burning under the relentless sun.
My dark tail flicks away the flies
That crawl across my face, biting me.
My light brown fur has shortened
In the coming of summer.
My tired legs quiver.
I long for a creek to drink from,
Or a tree to rest under.

On the horizon two figures appear.
The men have come to hurt me again.
As they draw closer, I can see
They are holding the hard ropes and whips.
My ears fall back against my skull,
I whinny in fear.

The men come even closer,
I paw the rough dusty ground with my hoof,
Warning them to stay away.
They snarl and grunt in their own language,
Their ugly hairless faces frowning at me.

I know I cannot face their whips again,
I retreat, galloping toward the burning sun,
Leaving a trail of dust clouding the air behind me.

Berlin Hill wrote the poem "A Lone Horse" when she was 11 years old, and it was chosen for publication by The Poetry Institute of Canada. The horse sculpture, Red Salutations by Al Glann, inspired Berlin's poem and her sketch. Artist Al Glann gladly gave permission for Berlin's drawing to appear in this book.

About the Author

Rosalee Klopf Tithof is now enjoying her hobby of writing children's stories after retiring from her rewarding years as a secondary education teacher. She earned her bachelor's degree at Saginaw Valley State University and later studied in Mexico City. She taught school for a year in a U.S. State Department School in Torreon, Mexico, a year that her whole family agreed was one of the best of their lives. She finished her career teaching in Chesaning, Michigan.

Her first book, *My Michigan Summer,* was published as an ebook and republished as a paperback book early in 2017 on Amazon. Her second book, *Remembering Pop Pop*, is also available on Amazon along with *Dancing with Great Grandma, I'll Love You Forever...Please Remember,* and now *Love Those Animals.* Each of these last four books highlight a grandchild. Rose spends winters in the Southwest and summers in Michigan.

Thank you to Julie Wenzlick for her expert editing skills and preparation of the text and illustrations for publication.

Also, a big thank you to talented designer Fred Arndt, who served as a consultant for me and for the illustrator, Carilyn. His expertise in perspective and eye for detail were much appreciated!

About the Illustrator

Carilyn Teichman is from Owosso, Michigan. She graduated from the Art Institue of Pittsburgh with a degree in Fashion Illustration in 1980. She has over 30 years of experience as a professional illustrator, which includes working as an illustrator in an advertising department and as an artist at a collectibles company. She worked at a sports-wear company, where her designs were embroidered on clothing and as an artist for a silkscreen printer.

Carilyn has illustrated paper doll sets for Pratt & Austin and paper dolls for magazines such as Contemporary Doll Collector Magazine and Miniature Collector. She also illustrated the children's books, *Remembering Pop Pop, Dancing with Great Grandma, I'll Love You Forever...Please Remember,* and *Duke the Legend.*

Credits

Los Angeles Zoo, 5333 Zoo Drive, Los Angeles, CA 90027

The Living Desert Zoo and Gardens, 47900 Portola Ave., Palm Desert, CA 92260

sheldrickwildlifetrust.org, Nairobi, Kenya, Nairobi National Park

Jane Goodall Institute, janegoodall.org, 1595 Spring Hill Rd., Suite 550, Vienna, VA 22182

J.K. Rowling, c/o Bloomsbury Publishing PLC, 50 Bedford Square, London WC 1B 3DP, UK

Al Glann/Sculptor, alglannsculptor.com

www.ingramcontent.com/pod-product-compliance
Lightning Source LLC
Chambersburg PA
CBHW042118040426
42449CB00002B/90